0400120

P9-DDZ-226

ON LINE

JBIOG
Truma
Gaines, Ann Graham

Harry S. Truman : our thirty-third president

HARRY S. *Truman*

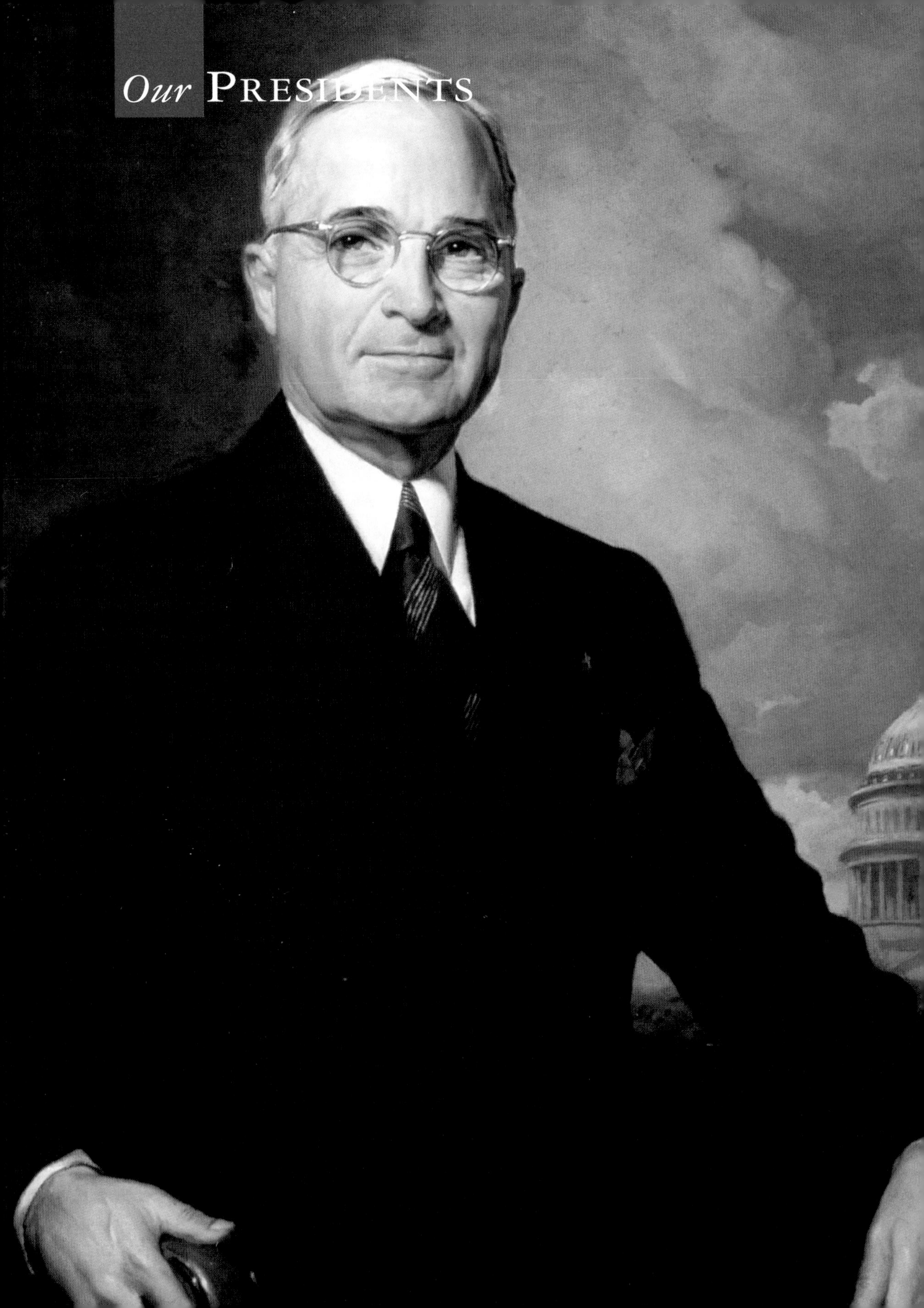

HARRY S. *Truman*

OUR THIRTY-THIRD PRESIDENT

By Ann Graham Gaines

SPIRIT
of America®

The Child's World®
Chanhassen, Minnesota

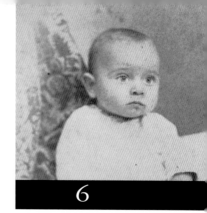

6

HARRY S. *Truman*

Published in the United States of America by The Child's World®
PO Box 326 • Chanhassen, MN 55317-0326 • 800-599-READ • www.childsworld.com

Acknowledgments

The Creative Spark: Mary Francis-DeMarois, Project Director; Elizabeth Sirimarco Budd, Series Editor;
Robert Court, Design and Art Direction; Janine Graham, Page Layout; Jennifer Moyers, Production

The Child's World®, Inc.: Mary Berendes, Publishing Director; Red Line Editorial, Fact Research;
Cindy Klingel, Curriculum Advisor; Robert Noyed, Historical Advisor

Photos

Cover, 2, 22: White House Collection, courtesy White House Historical Association. Bettmann/Corbis:
37; Library of Congress: 30. The following images are courtesy of the Harry S. Truman Library with
copyright holder as noted: Department of State: 33; *Kansas City Star:* 10; National Park Service
Photograph, Abbie Rowe: 19, 23, 26; Harry S. Truman Library: 6, 7, 11, 12, 13, 14, 15, 16, 31, 35, 36;
U.S. Army Signal Corps 25, 28, 29.

Registration

The Child's World®, Spirit of America®, and their associated logos are the sole property and
registered trademarks of The Child's World®.

Library of Congress Cataloging-in-Publication Data

Gaines, Ann.
  Harry S. Truman : our thirty-third president / by Ann Graham Gaines.
    p. cm.
  Includes bibliographical references (p.) and index.
  ISBN 1-56766-867-4 (lib. bdg. : alk. paper)
    1. Truman, Harry S., 1884–1972—Juvenile literature. 2. Presidents—United States—Biography—
Juvenile literature. [1. Truman, Harry S., 1884–1972. 2. Presidents.] I. Title.
  E814 .G35 2001
  973.918'092—dc21

                                    00-013165

13   29   36

Contents

Chapter ONE

Young Truman

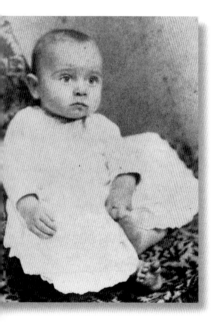

Harry S. Truman was born in Lamar, Missouri, on May 8, 1884. He became the nation's 33rd president in 1945 after the death of Franklin D. Roosevelt.

HARRY S. TRUMAN WAS ELECTED VICE president of the United States in 1944. He expected to serve his **term** and then return to the U.S. Senate. He thought Americans would then elect someone else to replace Franklin Delano Roosevelt, who was beginning his fourth term as president. Instead, just a few weeks after being sworn in as vice president, Truman found himself taking a new oath of office on April 12, 1945. Roosevelt had unexpectedly died that afternoon. When a U.S. president dies, the vice president steps into office. Thus, Truman found himself in a job for which he felt unprepared. During his presidency, some Americans criticized him. Today, however, many historians consider him one of the greatest presidents.

6

Harry S. Truman rose to fame from humble beginnings. He was born on May 8, 1884, in Lamar, Missouri. Harry's father, John, earned his living by selling livestock, such as horses and mules. The fenced lot where he kept the animals sat just across the street from their house. This allowed John to spend a lot of time with his family. Harry's mother, Martha, took care of their home. This was not easy because their house had no electricity or running water. She cooked on a wood stove and did their laundry outside in a tub.

The Truman family lived in this small, plain house in Lamar, Missouri, when Harry was born.

Interesting Facts

▶ The Truman home was a popular place among the children of their neighborhood. They could pet horses or hitch goats to the wagon Harry's father had built.

Harry Truman's father, John Anderson Truman, was born in 1851. Harry's mother, Martha Ellen Young Truman, was born in 1852. In the 1840s, both of their families had moved from Kentucky to Westport, Missouri.

The Trumans had many relatives living in Missouri. Harry's grandparents, aunts, uncles, and cousins all lived in the same area. They visited each other often. Soon Harry also had a brother, Vivian, and a sister, Mary Jane.

Martha Truman was an educated woman with a college degree. She taught Harry to read before he was five years old. She did not think the schools in their town were good enough for her children. Martha wanted them to attend the bigger and better schools in the town of Independence. In 1890, the family moved there.

In Independence, the Trumans bought a big house on a huge lot. John Truman went back to selling livestock. He also continued to do some farming. He dug a vegetable garden at their new home. Martha's father had died, leaving the Truman family his farm. John Truman continued to grow crops there, going back and forth between their house in the city and the farm in the country.

Harry enjoyed starting school in Independence. Just as his mother had hoped, he always did well in his classes and loved to read. By nature, he was a quiet boy. He admitted later that he was "kind of a sissy." Even so, he made many friends. By the time he was in high school, Harry had formed a strong friendship with Bess Wallace, a young woman he had met when he was just five years old. They graduated together in 1901. By that time, Harry had grown to his full size. At five feet ten inches tall, he was a slim man with a ready smile.

Soon after high school, Harry had to move away. John Truman had lost a great deal of money in a bad business deal. The Truman family had to sell their house in Independence. They moved to Kansas City in 1902 so John could take a new job. Harry had hoped to go to college, but now his family did not have enough money for it. So after high school, he worked first for the Santa Fe Railroad and then as a bank clerk. In 1906, his father asked him to help run the farm where he worked.

Interesting Facts

▶ John and Martha Truman named their son Harry S. Truman. They never decided what the S. would stand for. Martha's father thought it stood for his name, Solomon. John's father thought it stood for Shippe, his middle name. Harry Truman never took either name, preferring to use just the initial.

▶ As a boy, Harry loved to listen to stories his grandfather told. These tales of adventure were about his experiences leading trains of covered wagons over rugged trails from Missouri to the West.

Harry had bad eyesight and needed thick glasses to be able to see well. "Without my glasses, I was as blind as a bat," he once said. The glasses were so expensive that his mother would not allow him to play rough sports. "I was kind of a sissy," Truman recalled.

Harry Truman hated the life of a farmer, but he devoted 10 years to it because he wanted to please his father. In his free time, he served in the National Guard, the volunteer branch of the U.S. Army. He also traveled back to Independence to see his old friend Bess Wallace. When John Truman died in 1914, Harry continued to work on the farm, but he looked for other work as well.

World War I broke out in Europe in 1914. When the United States entered the war in 1917, Harry Truman joined the army. He believed it was the duty of the United States to help Great Britain, France, and Russia fight Germany. He thought Germany must be stopped from expanding into an ever-more-powerful empire. Truman had always liked to study the history of war. In the army, he could use what he had learned.

Just before he left, Truman proposed to Bess. She agreed to marry him when he came

Interesting Facts

▶ Truman started to wear glasses when he was just five years old.

▶ Truman cheated on his eye exam to get into the army by memorizing the eye chart. He remembered he was "stirred in heart and soul" by the war and wanted so desperately to fight that he was willing to do anything to join the military.

home from the war. In France, Truman served as an **officer.** His troops included tough men who liked to look for trouble, but they obeyed Truman. He was a good commander, and his men fought bravely.

Harry Truman met Elizabeth Virginia Wallace, his future wife, at Sunday school when they were young children. Bess, as she was nicknamed, was born in Independence, Missouri, on February 13, 1885. This made her nine months younger than Harry.

Harry and Bess Wallace went to school together. She was a very active little girl. A friend remembered that Bess was the first girl she ever knew who could whistle through her teeth. Bess loved to ice-skate and play baseball and tennis. Harry wasn't nearly as good at sports as Bess was. He preferred to read or play piano, and his glasses made him look quiet and studious. Occasionally, Bess allowed Harry to carry her books home from school. Sometimes they studied together. But in school, they were just friends, even if Harry thought she was the prettiest girl in town.

Bess and Harry graduated from high school in 1901. She then went to a school for women in Kansas City. But when her father died in 1903, she returned home to be with her mother. Together with her three brothers, they moved into her grandfather's house. For the next 16 years, Bess helped her mother run the household. Then one day, Harry Truman took a trip to Independence. He and Bess renewed their friendship. They would see each other whenever possible until 1917, when they finally became engaged. They married when Harry returned from World War I in 1919.

When Bess Truman became the first lady, many Americans said she was the woman they most admired. She donated her time to many charitable causes.

12

She was a quiet, gracious hostess, but she did not hold press conferences or grant interviews with reporters. Mrs. Truman always worked hard to be a good **politician's** wife. Even so, she was glad when her husband decided not to run for a third term as president. She could hardly wait to return to a quiet life in Missouri.

Mrs. Truman reached an older age than any other first lady in history. She died in October of 1982 at the age of 97. In a show of admiration, three other first ladies attended her funeral: Nancy Reagan, Rosalynn Carter, and Betty Ford.

Chapter TWO

A Start in Politics

Truman fought bravely during World War I. He served for nearly two years before he was discharged in 1919.

WHEN WORLD WAR I WAS OVER, TRUMAN returned to Missouri. Bess was happy to have him home, and they married immediately. They had already agreed that farming was not the life for them. It had provided a living for Truman for a long time, but he had never liked the work. Bess did not want to live in the country and do a lot of farm chores.

So with Bess's support, Truman went into business with a friend, Eddie Jacobson. They opened a haberdashery, a men's clothing store, in Kansas City. But in 1921, thousands of businesses failed. Truman and Jacobson's store was one of these. The failure left Truman $12,000 in **debt.** It would take him 15 years to pay back what he owed.

14

Truman opened a men's store with his friend Edward Jacobson. It was located on 12th Street in Kansas City, Missouri.

It was at this point that Truman began his career in politics, the work of the government. In those days, county judges in Missouri did not work in courts. Instead, they were leaders who helped manage the county government. They were in charge of hiring county workers. They also decided when to build or fix county property, such as the courthouse or roads and streets. In March of 1922, Truman became a **candidate** in the election for judge of the eastern **district** of Jackson County, where Kansas City is located. He won this election by 300 votes. Truman soon gained a reputation for being honest and forthright.

15

Later Truman said that he won his first election thanks to his many relatives who lived in the county. But it was really a large group of war **veterans** who first encouraged him to run. Truman also won support from leaders of the local Democratic Party, one of the two major U.S. **political parties.**

In February of 1924, the Trumans' daughter, Margaret, was born. She would be their only child. Unfortunately, they experienced disappointment later that year when Truman did not win reelection to his position as judge. He lost because he had angered the many members of Missouri's Democratic Party who belonged to the Ku Klux Klan. The Ku Klux Klan is a secret organization that believes white people are superior to members of other races. Members of the Klan had a lot of political power in Missouri during the 1920s. While he was a judge, Truman had spoken out against them many times when they threatened African Americans. Klan members sometimes tried to scare families into moving away by setting fire to their property. They also tried to keep African Americans from voting.

16

After losing the election, Truman took different jobs. He worked for the Automobile Club of Kansas and then for a savings and loan association. He studied law as well. In 1926, he won election to the office of judge once again. By this time, the Ku Klux Klan had lost some of its power.

The people of Truman's community especially appreciated his work during the Great Depression. This was a period in U.S. history when there was little business activity. Many people could not find work. "During that period," Truman once said, "I had to make work projects and build roads and buildings … to keep enough people employed in the county so nobody would starve."

He filled the office of county judge until 1934, when he was elected a U.S. senator. The family moved to Washington, D.C., in time for Bess and Margaret to watch him take his oath of office in January of 1935. In the Senate, Truman became known as a plain but honest man who spoke his mind. He was easily reelected in 1940.

During his second term as senator, Truman became known to people all over the country.

World War II had broken out in Europe after Germany invaded Poland. Soon Italy and Japan entered the war on Germany's side. Americans argued about whether the United States should fight. To be ready for any decision, the country began to prepare for war. As it turned out, it was fortunate that it did so. The Japanese bombed Pearl Harbor in Hawaii on December 7, 1941. The following day, the United States declared war on Japan.

Earlier that year, Harry Truman had been appointed head of a special Senate committee that investigated how the **Defense Department** spent its money. He later discovered that some officials had been cheating both before and during the war. They had allowed certain companies to overcharge the military for weapons. Truman was credited with saving the nation millions of dollars. *Time* magazine ran his photo on its cover, declaring him its "Man of the Year" in 1943.

By 1944, Franklin Delano Roosevelt had already served three terms as president. He needed a vice presidential candidate and asked Truman to accept this opportunity. Roosevelt knew Truman was admired by most Americans,

as well as by other politicians. A vice presidential candidate with enemies would have made it more difficult for Roosevelt to win. Truman was a safe choice, and with his help, Roosevelt easily won election to a fourth term. The **inauguration** took place on January 20. The event was a solemn occasion, for the United States had been at war for more than three years.

Truman began to settle into his new job as vice president. He seldom saw President

The Democratic Party chose Truman as its vice presidential candidate on July 21, 1944. He and President Roosevelt won the election on November 7 and spoke to reporters about their plans.

Roosevelt, who was busy dealing with the war. The president also was attending secret meetings with his military advisors, who were hard at work directing the creation of an **atomic bomb.** This extremely powerful weapon would be capable of terrible destruction. Roosevelt and his aides worried that Germany was hard at work on a similar weapon. They believed the United States needed to have one to ensure that it would not lose the war.

Just as Truman began to settle into his new position, everything changed. On April 12, 1945, he spent a long day doing his job as vice president, **presiding** over the Senate. Just a few minutes before five o'clock in the afternoon, the Senate meeting ended. Truman then visited the office of his friend, Congressman Sam Rayburn. Rayburn had received a message asking Truman to telephone the White House immediately. When he called, President Roosevelt's secretary asked Truman to go to the White House at once. When he arrived, he was taken to see President Roosevelt's wife, Eleanor. She broke the news to Truman at once: Franklin Roosevelt had died that afternoon. His health had been failing, but no one was prepared for his death.

20

IN JANUARY OF 1945, FRANKLIN DELANO ROOSEVELT BEGAN HIS FOURTH TERM as president. He was very popular with most Americans because he had helped the nation recover from the Great Depression with what he called his "New Deal." The New Deal programs helped millions of Americans by creating jobs and providing assistance to the unemployed.

When World War II began, Roosevelt became a world leader. He met with Winston Churchill of Great Britain and Joseph Stalin of the **Soviet Union.** The three men planned the strategy that would help the **Allies** win the war against Germany, Italy, and Japan. Americans gained new admiration for Roosevelt. What they did not realize was that his health had begun to worsen. In the early 1920s, he had been struck with a disease called polio. He spent the rest of his life in a wheelchair or using braces to help him walk. For a long time, Roosevelt's health was stable. But by his fourth inauguration, he felt tired and weak. He went to Warm Springs, Georgia, where he had established a center for people with polio. There, just three months after taking the oath of office, he died. Americans had no warning that he was so ill. They were shocked and expressed great sorrow over his death, for he had skillfully led the nation during difficult times.

Chapter THREE

President Truman

Truman planned only to serve a single term as vice president and then return to the Senate, but fate changed his future when President Roosevelt died.

TWO MINUTES AFTER HARRY TRUMAN LEARNED he would be president, radios broadcast the news to the American public. All the members of Roosevelt's **cabinet** gathered at the White House. So did leaders of Congress. Truman called Bess and Margaret to come at once, and at 7:09 PM, he took the oath of office. That night, he held his first cabinet meeting. Afterward, he met in private with the secretary of war. He learned for the first time about the atomic bomb.

Truman felt afraid and unprepared. But he knew Americans were counting on him, and he set to work. As president, he typically woke up early in the morning. He started the day with a walk, a massage, and breakfast. He was in his office by seven o'clock each morning.

U.S. relations with other countries held most of Truman's attention at the beginning of his presidency. Less than two weeks after he took the oath of office, an important meeting took place. Fifty countries gathered in San Francisco to organize the United Nations. The goals of this organization were to help maintain peace and to create better relations between

Harry S. Truman took the oath of office on April 12, 1945, after the death of Franklin D. Roosevelt. Truman was nervous about his new leadership role. He felt that he was not prepared for such a great responsibility.

countries. Truman devoted a great deal of effort to convincing voters that the United States should join. The United Nations came into being later that year, in October of 1945. The United States and most of the other 50 nations agreed to the organization's principles.

But military matters took up even more of Truman's time. When he became president, World War II was already in its fourth year. Just weeks after Roosevelt died, Germany **surrendered.** This meant the war was over in Europe, but it raged on in Japan. President Truman represented the United States at the Potsdam Conference, where Allied leaders met to discuss how to deal with defeated Germany. He met Winston Churchill, prime minister of Great Britain, and Joseph Stalin, the Soviet Union's leader. They agreed that the Allies should work together to govern Germany. They divided the country into four zones.

Germany surrendered less than a month after Truman became president. That summer, he met with Generals Dwight D. Eisenhower (left) and George Patton (center) in Berlin to celebrate the Allied victory.

Truman met with Premier Joseph Stalin (left) and Prime Minister Winston Churchill (right) at the Potsdam Conference in July and August of 1945.

Britain, France, the Soviet Union, and the United States would each be responsible for one zone.

Japan continued fighting the Allies in the Pacific, but it was growing weaker. The Allies sent messages to Japan demanding its surrender. But its emperor would not agree. Truman learned that at least 100,000 more Americans might lose their lives before Japan could be conquered. Reluctantly, he decided that the United States should use its atomic bomb to end the war and save American lives. This was a difficult decision. He knew that using the bomb would cause terrible death and destruction.

On July 26, 1945, President Truman delivered an **ultimatum** to the Japanese. He told them that if they did not surrender, Japan would face complete destruction. "If they do not now accept our terms, they may expect a rain of ruin from the air the like of which has never been seen on this earth," he warned.

The Japanese did not know about the atomic bomb. They saw no reason to surrender. So on August 6, the United States bombed the city of Hiroshima. The bomb destroyed more than four square miles of the city and brought death or injury to many thousands of Japanese citizens. Still, the emperor refused to give up. A second bomb was dropped on the city of Nagasaki three days later. Finally, the emperor surrendered on August 14.

By the end of World War II, new problems were developing in other parts of the world. One was the rise of **communism,** which is a system for running a government. In communist countries, citizens do not own land and businesses. Instead, everything is owned by the government and belongs to the country as a whole. The Soviet Union had been a communist country since 1917.

26

President Truman liked to meet the American people whenever he could. Here he is shown (seated at left) with members of the Boy Scouts of America.

Its leaders believed that all farms and factories belonged to the government. Communist leaders believed in an all-powerful state with only one political party. The Soviet people did not have elections. They also had no personal freedoms, such as freedom of speech or the freedom to practice religion.

After World War II, the Soviet Union planned to spread communism to other parts of the world. It **occupied** Eastern Europe and set up communist governments in many countries there. Soon the Soviet Union became a powerful empire. This power and the communist ideals posed a threat to **democracies.**

Relations between the Soviet Union and the other Allies had begun to fall apart even

27

before the war ended. Afterward they became much more tense. The competitive and distrustful feelings between the Western democracies and the Soviet Union became known as the Cold War. Hoping to slow the spread of communism, Truman established the Truman Doctrine in 1947. This was a promise that the United States would lend support to any country threatened by communism.

Much of Truman's first term was dedicated to foreign relations—the nation's dealings with other countries.

WHEN HARRY TRUMAN BECAME president, it seemed likely that if the Allies invaded Japan, they would defeat this powerful enemy and end World War II. But Truman knew an invasion would cause the death of many thousands of Allied soldiers and sailors. He decided to use the atomic bomb.

A U.S. warplane dropped the bomb on the city of Hiroshima on August 6, 1945. The bomb exploded while still in the air. Witnesses will remember forever the sudden white flash. The earth shook. A cloud of dust created darkness. In less than a minute, 70,000 buildings were destroyed. More than 75,000 people died instantly. Another 60,000 would die before the year was over from burns, wounds, and sickness. A few days later, a second bomb was dropped on Nagasaki, with the same devastating effects.

At the time, many Americans expressed their belief that Truman had done the right thing by dropping the bomb. They praised him for having forced the Japanese to surrender. Today, however, the bombing of Hiroshima is remembered as one of the most horrible events in all of human history.

Chapter FOUR

A Second Term

As Truman's first term came to a close, he made plans to help the average American. But Republicans in Congress made it difficult for him to achieve these goals. Truman began to call his opponents the "do-nothing Congress."

TOWARD THE END OF HIS FIRST TERM, TRUMAN was able to devote more attention to problems at home. He knew that African American soldiers had been treated badly during and after the war. This angered him. He spoke out to encourage the government to create a new **civil rights** program. Truman wanted African Americans in the army to be treated fairly, and he wanted all African Americans to be guaranteed the right to vote. At the time, some people tried to stop black citizens from voting, especially in southern states. Truman also hoped to provide African Americans with better employment opportunities.

Truman wanted to help other Americans as well. He developed what he called his "Fair Deal" program. He hoped it would help

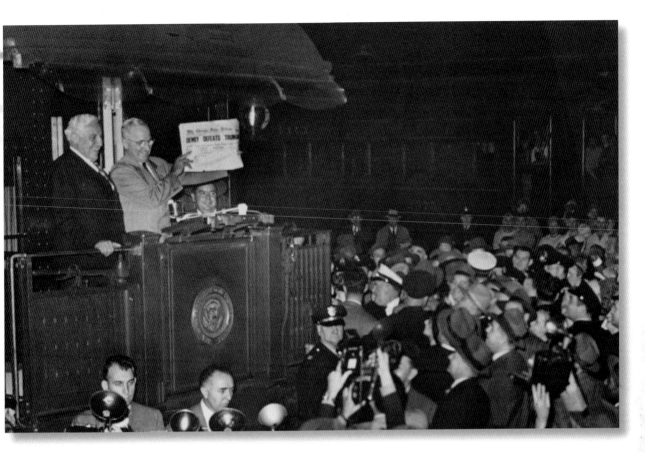

Americans by creating jobs and providing less expensive housing for people in need. He hoped to clean up the nation's slums and to provide health care to all Americans. Unfortunately, many members of Congress did not agree with President Truman's plans. They would not pass the necessary laws to make the Fair Deal program a success.

In 1948, Truman ran for election to a second term. By this time, he was not very popular with the American people. He was criticized for not getting anything done. It

The early edition of the Chicago Tribune proclaimed that Thomas Dewey had won the election of 1948. But victories in California and Ohio turned the tide. Truman won the election and posed with the incorrect headline.

31

▶ Before President Truman authorized other repairs to the White House, he had a balcony built on the outside of the mansion, behind the pillars on its south side. Many Americans complained because it changed the building's appearance. But Truman really liked it, partly because it offered shade to the downstairs rooms.

▶ The United States has governed the island of Puerto Rico since the end of the 19th century. In 1950, two Puerto Rican men attempted to murder President Truman. They wanted to advance the cause for Puerto Rican independence from the United States.

seemed as if the Democratic Party might not even **nominate** him as their candidate. But Truman was determined not to let that happen. He won back the support of many Democrats by taking a tough stand against their opponents, the Republicans. He attacked the Republicans in Congress, saying they were not doing their job. He called them the "do-nothing Congress" because they had **enacted** almost no laws.

The Republicans nominated Thomas E. Dewey to run against President Truman. The race was hard-fought. Truman went all over the country to speak to Americans, asking for their votes. He delivered 275 speeches. As the election drew to a close, the polls said Dewey would win. When the results came in, Truman was ahead. But some newspapers still announced Dewey's victory. Truman had actually defeated his opponent by a small number of votes, and on January 20, 1949, his inauguration took place.

During Truman's second term, the world remained in turmoil. Communism continued to spread. The Soviet Union had blocked all traffic in and out of the city of Berlin, hoping to place the city under communist control. Truman organized the Berlin Airlift to help the people of Berlin. Cargo planes from the United States and Great Britain dropped food, coal, and other supplies to the Berliners.

In 1950, the Korean War began. Communist North Korea attacked democratic South Korea. Soon China entered the war on the side of the communists. The countries of the United Nations (UN) entered on the side of South Korea. General Douglas MacArthur commanded the UN forces. Truman and MacArthur disagreed about how to handle the war. Truman did not want the United

General MacArthur (right) was in charge of United Nations troops during the Korean War. At first, he had great success. But when China joined the war on the side of communist North Korea, many American lives were lost. MacArthur wanted to wage war against China, but Truman did not agree. He finally removed MacArthur from his post.

▶ In 1951, Congress decided that no president should hold office for more than two terms. The 22nd **Amendment** was added to the U.S. **Constitution** that year. It stated, "No person shall be elected to the office of president more than twice." It also limited the amount of time that a vice president who took office during the elected president's term could hold office. It did make a special arrangement for President Truman, however. The amendment was written so that it did not take effect until the following president took office.

States to become involved in war with either the Soviet Union or China. Finally, in April of 1951, he removed MacArthur from his position. Truman believed MacArthur was making the conflict worse. The American public thought this was a terrible mistake, and Truman's popularity declined.

The fear of communism was perhaps the most talked-about issue of Truman's second term. Senator Joseph McCarthy began a "witch hunt" during that time. He was searching for communists living in the United States. Some Americans believed that communism was a good idea. Some even had joined the Communist Party. McCarthy wanted to find out who these people were. He established a Senate committee for this purpose. The committee accused many people, including politicians, writers, and actors, of being communists. Today historians realize that the committee made many false accusations, and that many of the people who actually did belong to the Communist Party posed no threat to American democracy.

As Truman's second term approached its end, he had to decide whether to run in the

next election. Although by this time, the U.S. Constitution limited presidents to only two terms, Truman's case was different. This new law would not take effect until the next president took office, so Truman could seek another full term. He decided against it, however. He told Americans that he would not run for a third term. "I do not think it is my duty to spend another four years in the White House," he said.

Republican Dwight D. Eisenhower, a hero from World War II, won the election of 1952. As he entered office, the Cold War

On July 6, 1957, the Trumans took part in the dedication of the Harry S. Truman Library in Independence, Missouri. Bess Truman is at left, and Eleanor Roosevelt is next to her. Harry Truman is at far right, and another former president, Herbert Hoover, stands third from right.

From 1953 until 1955, Truman worked on his memoirs. The first volume, Year of Decisions, *was published in November of 1955. The second volume,* Years of Trial and Hope, *appeared the following year.*

with the Soviet Union continued. Both the United States and the Soviet Union built huge supplies of weapons, preparing to fight at a moment's notice. For many years, people in both countries were afraid that deadly bombs would one day cause widespread destruction and death.

Truman was glad to retire. He and Bess moved back to Missouri to lead a quiet life. They spent time with family and old friends. They traveled to Europe twice, where they met with leaders including Winston Churchill and Pope Pius XII. The former president worked on writing his memoirs, the story of his life. He also supported Democratic candidates such as John F. Kennedy, who ran for president in 1960. Twenty years after leaving office, Harry S. Truman died at home on December 26, 1972. He was 88 years old.

Although Truman left office as an unpopular president, his reputation has been restored in recent years. Many historians now consider him one of the greatest presidents of all time, a man who stepped into office and worked hard to keep peace.

AFTER WORLD WAR II ENDED, Harry Truman had time to pay more attention to matters at home. One thing he couldn't help but notice was that the White House was falling apart. Pipes leaked. Walls crumbled and even fell down. Visitors to the second floor were lucky that the floor did not collapse beneath them! President Truman asked Congress to set aside an enormous amount of money to repair the president's home.

In 1948, he and his family moved to Blair House, a mansion located nearby. Workmen removed everything from the White House, including floors, mantels, doors, and furniture. Only the walls were left. Inside, a new steel skeleton was constructed. Then workers started to put the rooms back together. The entire project took more than three years. When the Truman family returned in March of 1952, the White House was once more elegant, beautiful, and safe. In the photograph above, Truman takes the American people on a televised tour of the restored White House with news reporter Walter Cronkite.

37

1884 Harry S. Truman is born on May 8, in Lamar, Missouri, to John and Martha Truman.

1890 The Truman family moves to Independence, Missouri.

1901 Truman graduates from high school.

1902 The Truman family moves from Independence to Kansas City. Harry goes to work for a railroad and then for a bank.

1905 Truman joins the National Guard. He serves until 1911.

1906 Truman begins working on a farm.

1914 World War I begins in Europe.

1917 When the United States enters World War I, Truman joins the army and goes to fight in Europe.

1919 Truman returns from the war. After he and Bess Wallace marry, he opens a men's clothing store.

1921 Truman's business fails.

1922 Friends encourage Truman to run for county judge. He wins the election.

1924 The Trumans' only child, Margaret, is born. Harry Truman is not reelected to his post as county judge.

1926 Truman is elected county judge once again.

1934 In November, Truman is elected to the U.S. Senate.

1939 World War II begins when Germany invades Poland. Great Britain and France fight Germany and its allies, Italy and Japan.

1940 Truman is reelected to the Senate.

1941 Japan bombs U.S. Navy ships at Pearl Harbor, Hawaii, on December 7. The United States enters World War II the next day, siding with Great Britain. Truman heads an investigation into Defense Department spending. He later learns that weapons companies have been cheating the government out of millions of dollars.

1943 *Time* magazine names Truman its "Man of the Year."

1944 Franklin Delano Roosevelt is reelected to a fourth term as president. Truman is elected vice president.

1945 On April 12, President Roosevelt dies. Truman is sworn in as the new president of the United States. In July, Truman goes to Europe to meet with other leaders at a conference at Potsdam, Germany. On August 6, he orders the atomic bomb dropped on the city of Hiroshima in Japan; a few days later, a bomb is dropped on Nagasaki. Japan surrenders on August 14.

1946 The Cold War begins after World War II as the former allies, the United States and Soviet Union, come into conflict.

1947 Truman establishes the Truman Doctrine, making a promise that the United States will help other democratic nations threatened by communism.

1948 Truman runs for reelection. Newspapers report that he has lost to Thomas E. Dewey, but Truman wins a second term. In June, the Soviet Union blocks supplies from getting to West Berlin. Truman orders the Berlin Airlift in which supplies such as food and coal are dropped to the Berliners from cargo planes.

1950 The Korean War begins. American soldiers fight on the side of democratic South Korea against invaders from communist North Korea.

1951 Truman loses popularity after he removes General Douglas MacArthur from his command of troops in Korea.

1952 Truman decides not to run for reelection. Dwight D. Eisenhower wins the election in November.

1953 Harry and Bess Truman retire to Missouri, where they lead a quiet life.

1972 Harry S. Truman dies on December 26 at age 88.

allies (AL-lize)
Allies are nations that have agreed to help each other by fighting together against a common enemy. During World War II, France, Great Britain, the Soviet Union, and the U.S. were known as the Allies.

amendment (uh-MEND-ment)
An amendment is a change or addition made to the U.S. Constitution or other documents. The 22nd Amendment states that no president can hold office for more than two terms.

atomic bomb (uh-TOM-ik BAWM)
An atomic bomb is a weapon that explodes with tremendous destructive power. The United States secretly developed atomic bombs during World War II.

cabinet (KAB-ih-net)
A cabinet is the group of people who advise a president. Truman held his first meeting with members of his cabinet on April 12, 1945.

candidate (KAN-dih-det)
A candidate is a person running in an election. In 1922, Truman was a candidate in an election for county judge.

civil rights (SIH-vel RYTZ)
Civil rights are the rights guaranteed by the U.S. Constitution to all citizens of the United States. Truman encouraged the government to create a new civil rights program.

communism (KOM-yeh-niz-em)
Communism is a system of government in which the central government, not the people, holds all the power. During the Cold War, a major goal of Soviet leaders was to spread communism throughout the world.

constitution (kon-stih-TOO-shun)
A constitution is the set of basic principles that govern a state, country, or society. The 22nd Amendment to the U.S. Constitution was approved in 1951.

debt (DET)
Debt is something that is owed. When Truman's business closed in 1921, he owed $12,000 in debt.

Defense Department (deh-FENS deh-PART-ment)
The Defense Department is the part of the national government that manages the military. While he was a senator, Truman investigated how the Defense Department spent its money.

democracies (deh-MOK-ruh-seez)
Democracies are countries in which the government is run by the people who live there. The United States is a democracy.

district (DIS-trikt)
A district is a small area. Truman was a candidate in the 1922 election for judge of the eastern district of Jackson County, Missouri.

enact (en-AKT)
To enact means to make a bill into a law. Truman believed that Congress did not enact enough laws.

inauguration (ih-nawg-yuh-RAY-shun)
An inauguration is the ceremony that takes place when a new president begins a term. Truman's inauguration took place on January 20, 1949.

nominate (NOM-ih-nayt)
When a political party nominates someone, it chooses that person to run for a political office. Truman worried that Democrats might not nominate him for the election of 1948.

occupied (AHK-yeh-pied)
An occupied area or country is one that has been taken over by another country. The Soviet Union occupied Eastern Europe after World War II.

officer (AW-fih-ser)
An officer is a leader in the military who commands other soldiers. Truman was an officer in the U.S. Army.

political parties (puh-LIT-ih-kul PAR-teez)
Political parties are groups of people who share similar ideas about how to run a government. Truman was a member of the Democratic political party.

politician (pawl-ih-TISH-un)
A politician is a person who holds an office in government. Truman was a politician.

preside (preh-ZYD)
When people preside over something, they are in charge of it. The vice president presides over the Senate.

Soviet Union (SOH-vee-et YOON-yen)
The Soviet Union was a communist country that stretched from eastern Europe across Asia to the Pacific Ocean. It separated into several smaller countries in 1991.

surrender (suh-REN-dur)
If an army surrenders, it gives up to its enemy. Germany surrendered in 1945.

term (TERM)
A term is the length of time a politician can keep his or her position by law. A U.S. president's term of office is four years.

ultimatum (ul-tih-MAY-tum)
An ultimatum is a threat. Truman issued an ultimatum to Japan toward the end of World War II.

veterans (VET-ur-enz)
Veterans are people who have served in the military. Veterans of World War I supported Truman when he ran in the election for county judge.

Our PRESIDENTS

President	Birthplace	Life Dates	Term	Political Party	First Lady
George Washington	Virginia	1732–1799	1789–1797	None	Martha Dandridge Custis Washington
John Adams	Massachusetts	1735–1826	1797–1801	Federalist	Abigail Smith Adams
Thomas Jefferson	Virginia	1743–1826	1801–1809	Democratic-Republican	widower
James Madison	Virginia	1751–1836	1809–1817	Democratic-Republican	Dolley Payne Todd Madison
James Monroe	Virginia	1758–1831	1817–1825	Democratic-Republican	Elizabeth "Eliza" Kortright Monroe
John Quincy Adams	Massachusetts	1767–1848	1825–1829	Democratic-Republican	Louisa Catherine Johnson Adams
Andrew Jackson	South Carolina	1767–1845	1829–1837	Democrat	widower
Martin Van Buren	New York	1782–1862	1837–1841	Democrat	widower
William Henry Harrison	Virginia	1773–1841	1841	Whig	Anna Tuthill Symmes Harrison
John Tyler	Virginia	1790–1862	1841–1845	Whig	Letitia Christian Tyler Julia Gardiner Tyler
James Polk	North Carolina	1795–1849	1845–1849	Democrat	Sarah Childress Polk

Our PRESIDENTS

President	Birthplace	Life Dates	Term	Political Party	First Lady
Zachary Taylor	Virginia	1784–1850	1849–1850	Whig	Margaret Mackall Smith Taylor
Millard Fillmore	New York	1800–1874	1850–1853	Whig	Abigail Powers Fillmore
Franklin Pierce	New Hampshire	1804–1869	1853–1857	Democrat	Jane Means Appleton Pierce
James Buchanan	Pennsylvania	1791–1868	1857–1861	Democrat	never married
Abraham Lincoln	Kentucky	1809–1865	1861–1865	Republican	Mary Todd Lincoln
Andrew Johnson	North Carolina	1808–1875	1865–1869	Democrat	Eliza McCardle Johnson
Ulysses S. Grant	Ohio	1822–1885	1869–1877	Republican	Julia Dent Grant
Rutherford B. Hayes	Ohio	1822–1893	1877–1881	Republican	Lucy Ware Webb Hayes
James A. Garfield	Ohio	1831–1881	1881	Republican	Lucretia Rudolph Garfield
Chester A. Arthur	Vermont	1829–1886	1881–1885	Republican	widower
Grover Cleveland	New Jersey	1837–1908	1885–1889	Democrat	Frances Folsom Cleveland

Our PRESIDENTS

President	Birthplace	Life Dates	Term	Political Party	First Lady
Benjamin Harrison	Ohio	1833–1901	1889–1893	Republican	Caroline Lavina Scott Harrison
Grover Cleveland	New Jersey	1837–1908	1893–1897	Democrat	Frances Folsom Cleveland
William McKinley	Ohio	1843–1901	1897–1901	Republican	Ida Saxton McKinley
Theodore Roosevelt	New York	1858–1919	1901–1909	Republican	Edith Kermit Carow Roosevelt
William Howard Taft	Ohio	1857–1930	1909–1913	Republican	Helen Herron Taft
Woodrow Wilson	Virginia	1856–1924	1913–1921	Democrat	Ellen L. Axson Wilson Edith Bolling Galt Wilson
Warren G. Harding	Ohio	1865–1923	1921–1923	Republican	Florence Kling De Wolfe Harding
Calvin Coolidge	Vermont	1872–1933	1923–1929	Republican	Grace Anna Goodhue Coolidge
Herbert Hoover	Iowa	1874–1964	1929–1933	Republican	Lou Henry Hoover
Franklin D. Roosevelt	New York	1882–1945	1933–1945	Democrat	Anna Eleanor Roosevelt Roosevelt
Harry S. Truman	Missouri	1884–1972	1945–1953	Democrat	Elizabeth "Bess" Virginia Wallace Truman

Our PRESIDENTS

President	Birthplace	Life Dates	Term	Political Party	First Lady
Dwight D. Eisenhower	Texas	1890–1969	1953–1961	Republican	Mamie Geneva Doud Eisenhower
John F. Kennedy	Massachusetts	1917–1963	1961–1963	Democrat	Jacqueline Lee Bouvier Kennedy
Lyndon Baines Johnson	Texas	1908–1973	1963–1969	Democrat	Claudia "Lady Bird" Alta Taylor Johnson
Richard M. Nixon	California	1913–1994	1969–1974	Republican	Thelma "Pat" Catherine Patricia Ryan Nixon
Gerald R. Ford	Nebraska	1913–	1974–1977	Republican	Elizabeth "Betty" Bloomer Warren Ford
James Earl Carter	Georgia	1924–	1977–1981	Democrat	Rosalynn Smith Carter
Ronald Reagan	Illinois	1911–	1981–1989	Republican	Nancy Davis Reagan
George Bush	Massachusetts	1924–	1989–1993	Republican	Barbara Pierce Bush
William J. Clinton	Arkansas	1946–	1993–2001	Democrat	Hillary Rodham Clinton
George W. Bush	Connecticut	1946–	2001–	Republican	Laura Welch Bush

Qualifications

To run for president, a candidate must
• be at least 35 years old
• be a citizen who was born in the United States
• have lived in the United States for 14 years

Term of Office

A president's term of office is four years. No president can stay in office for more than two terms.

Election Date

The presidential election takes place every four years on the first Tuesday of November.

Inauguration Date

Presidents are inaugurated on January 20.

Oath of Office

I do solemnly swear I will faithfully execute the office of the President of the United States and will to the best of my ability preserve, protect, and defend the Constitution of the United States.

Write a Letter to the President

One of the best things about being a U.S. citizen is that Americans get to participate in their government. They can speak out if they feel government leaders aren't doing their jobs. They can also praise leaders who are going the extra mile. Do you have something you'd like the president to do? Should the president worry more about the environment and encourage people to recycle? Should the government spend more money on our schools? You can write a letter to the president to say how you feel!

1600 Pennsylvania Avenue
Washington, D.C. 20500

You can even send an e-mail to: president@whitehouse.gov

46

For Further INFORMATION

Internet Sites

Visit Harry S. Truman's home, which is now a National Historic Site:
http://www.nps.gov/hstr

View a digital archive that includes many photographs and documents from
Harry Truman's life:
http://www.whistlestop.org

Find out more about the meeting of Allied leaders at Potsdam:
http://www.trumanlibrary.org/teacher/potsdam.htm

Learn more about why Truman was reelected president in 1948 by reading "Harry S.
Truman: Fighter in a Fighting Year," from *Time* magazine:
http://www.time.com/time/special/moy/1948.html

Find out more about World War II:
http://grolier.com/wwii/wwii_2.html

Learn more about all the presidents and visit the White House:
http://www.whitehouse.gov/WH/glimpse/presidents/html/presidents.html
http://www.thepresidency.org/presinfo.htm
http://www.americanpresidents.org/

Books

Bowler, Sarah. *Dwight D. Eisenhower: Our Thirty-Fourth President.* Chanhassen, MN: The Child's World, 2002.

Feinberg, Barbara Silberdick. *Bess Wallace Truman.* New York: Childrens Press, 1999.

Feinstein, Stephen. *The 1950s from the Korean War to Elvis.* New Jersey: Enslow, 2000.

Maupin, Melissa. *Franklin D. Roosevelt: Our Thirty-Second President.* Chanhassen, MN: The Child's World, 2002.

Steins, Richard. *The Allies against the Axis: World War II (1940–1950).* New York: Twenty-First Century Books, 1995.

Warren, James A. *Cold War: The American Crusade against the Soviet Union and World Communism, 1945–1990.* New York: Lothrop, Lee & Shepard, 1996.

Index